time for paws

By Zoe Wilson

First published in the United Kingdom in 2013

Published by Resource

ISBN 978-0-9927290-0-4

Thank you to Jennie Franklin for the stunning photography of our friends.

For Timmi

I broke my Mummy's heart.
When I moved on her world fell apart
From that break in her heart, words started flowing
And now her love of writing is growing
Her heart never healed but re-learned how to love
Her two new friends who I watch out for from above...

contents

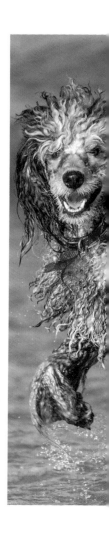

i had a thought

One day a little dog had a very big thought
How he'd like to get onto Centre Court
It's not about being a boy or a girl
I think a puppy should give it a whirl
One day on the park he took what he needed
Surely this tennis ball would get him seeded?
He followed the smells of strawberries and cream
Over road, lane, valley and stream
Through parks, estates, houses and trees
And finally arrived to the sound of 'new balls please'

it's after me

The faster I run the closer it gets
I'm not this scared when I go to the vets!
'Let's go to the beach Ron for a bit of fun'
Famous last words before my marathon run
The last thing I know I'm skipping in the sea
The next thing I know it's bearing down on me
My little legs are good at a trot
But this kind of pace is asking a lot!
This chase on the shore is getting out of hand
Can't you see I'm not built for the sand?
I gallop on just to stay out of reach
'Oh come on Ronnie, it's just your reflection on the beach!'

my
treats

This is my face – at all times of day
When people meet me they're not sure what to say
My expression is constant – this is me when I'm mad
And I look like this when I'm happy and sad!
I'm a gentle giant with a heart of gold
And attractive to some – or so I've been told
I eat like a horse and snack on the trot
At breakfast and dinner I eat quite a lot
But I don't need a lunchbox for a treat out on trips
As I've got a tasty stash in the corner of my lips!

the
chase

We run once a week and it's meant to be fun
But I really don't know why I bother to come
Is this sort of pairing something I need?
As it's simply unfair when it comes to our speed
She chases me around and I do play the part
If only she knew, I would give her my heart
We hang out together like butter wouldn't melt
And more than just once it's love that I've felt
I'm sure given time we could build on that love
After all look – we fit like a glove!
So Lily, Lily you know that I care –

– but please stop chasing me...

... I'm
not a
hare

it wasn't me

I can tell by your face that the evidence is there
But to blame me for this just isn't fair!
If I'd eaten him whole I'd have a big lump
And it did have wings and I can't jump!
The blame lies elsewhere, of that I am sure
I suspect it was the owner of more than one claw
So now you're to be my judge and jury
But find me guilty – you'll feel my Pug fury!
Lastly, I wish I'd put two and two together
And never ever, ever picked up this feather!

revenge

We come to the beach whenever we can
And to stay on the sand is always the plan
I behave at the start, and trot along like a saint
Tip toe, tip toe don't I look quaint?
I come off my rope and she says 'just behave'
A little late for that Mum – as I'm under a wave
Not that I meant to lead her astray
But when tied by that leash I just can't play
Before I dive in my fur is so neat
Styled straight and tidy from my head to my feet
My ribbon is soaked and my collar as well
And seawater stops the ding of my bell
My Mother is fuming – that is quite clear
But me – I'm still smiling from ear to ear
But sadly Mum says 'I've pushed it to the wire'
And takes her revenge with a brush and hairdryer!

the private

joke

You didn't see what I just saw
It involved the cat and its tail and a door
Don't think I'm being mean at Tabby's expense
But that cat treats me like I'm completely dense
If I ever catch Tabby when he's messing up
I laugh from my belly like I'm still a small pup!
It's good between us some of the time
I like his company and we can get on just fine
Tabby came first and me years after
Now the worst thing for him is to hear my laughter
The best one of all was when he slipped off the fence
Yes, I do like a laugh at Tabby's expense!

deflated

We all know it comes around every four years
And the name of it nearly brings me to tears
I lose my Daddy to a life of TV
Whatever I do he still ignores me!
His friends come around, and he acts like a loony,
And wear those shirts to look like Wayne Rooney
I know what I'll do – what a good call
I'll go and find his favourite football!
I approach very slowly from just underneath
And tap it, it falls and I sink in my teeth!
How strange, it is squealing, as if almost in pain
As I trot over to Daddy it squeals again
I sit and I wait for a look through the door
And when I see him I squeeze it some more
But why so angry – it's my bubble that burst
It's only a football – it could have been worse!
I think how I hate that dreadful World Cup
As he shouts – 'oh no, you naughty little pup'
Oh dear the dead ball is still shrinking and hissing
Is this my clue to take leave and go missing?

I'm from the

north east

In the hot summer weather I know where I'm from
But that all changes when winter comes along!
It's a matter of principle, identity and pride
But my master's dress code is not on my side!
It's clear I'm a Yorkie and from the North East
Not from over the border – or a big Scottish beast!
I know that this coat helps keep off the rain
But mistaken identity can be a real pain
When rain clouds approach I feel a change in my mood
And wearing this in public – well frankly it's rude
I know it's essential and storm clouds are scary
But must I really dress up like Julian Clary?
I'm proud I'm from Yorkshire, it's the way that I'm built
Whatever next – will they have me in a kilt?

clippers

Is that a knock I hear at the door?
I recognise the voice – it's her I am sure
As if I want to be all tidy and prim
I'm a boy after all and didn't need that last trim!
If I jump down now and run off to play
Do you think she'll lose interest and book another day?
I like to be shaggy and get wet and smell
I like to have a long dirty beard as well
So that's the plan – ignore her, she'll leave
But no she's still knocking – I just can't believe…
She's in the house and I can see her clippers
Why have I got fur – and not a pair of flippers?

the wish

I used to be bad – I have nothing to hide
Until Daddy got these tasty treats on his side
I lick and I look, and hold on with my paws
And chew and chew until I have cramp in my jaws
Before the reward – a different story to tell
It's fair to say that I made their life Hell!
Now I'm an angel in my favourite spot
It's hidden away, not too cold, not too hot
The ground is quite soft, so I can bury my stash
'Cause when Daddy calls he expects me to dash
My treat is special – it changed who I am
Now being good is part of my plan!
The best bit is the middle – tasty as a peach
If only, if only, if only I could reach
I've tried and tried and now it's getting late
I wish I had a tongue like the chap on page 28!

part
of
me

It is big and it's rosy and I use it every day
And without it I wouldn't be able to play
For all of my life it has lived on one side
And every day I wear it with pride
It keeps me going through days and nights
And helps me out in my fight or flights
It's bigger than most and some stop and stare
It's part of me and so I just don't care
It's fair to say that it plays a big part
And by now you all know that I'm talking about 'my heart'!

chinese

It was whispered in our ear, now we've got a secret!
We've stored it away and promised to keep it
Nobody else has heard it before
If it goes any further it'll cause a furore
It's about Lily's owners they were heard on the phone
Apparently they are all looking for a lovely new home
One with more room and a big long lawn
Where Lily can play from dusk till dawn

I promised not to tell – but in you I trust
It's a good one for sure, and worth all the fuss
I know you're discreet and not one to chat
It can't go any further – no, we can't have that!
It's about Lily's owners they were heard on the phone
Apparently they want to leave poor Lily 'alone'!

whispers

I know that it's windy so I'll have to shout
I haven't even met who this secret's about
Oh dear, my goodness you look very disturbed
But I promise this is it – exactly what I heard!
It's about Lily's owners they were heard on the phone
They're going to put her in an unwanted dog's home!

Hello there stranger – you look like you're fun
But I've got something to tell you before we run
It's about Lily's owners they were heard on the phone
They're going to put Lily in an old dog's home!
I heard it today and well, who'd credit that?
Yes, they're moving away and even taking the cat
Oh dear, you look sad – oh why would that be?

Because my little friend, that poor Lily
...is me!

listen

Why won't you listen, I know it is rude to shout
But this is the only way that I can get my words out
If it's a question of food or walkies time
I make myself clear – as barking's no crime
It doesn't stop there – I shout in a crowd
And that is when my voice is quite loud
I get looks and stares and 'what a bad Russell'
But I don't care as I flex my barking muscle!
Others' opinions are no great shakes
A good shout and a bark is all that it takes
I know that I look too rowdy to keep
But I'm very, very quiet – when I'm asleep!

the
catch

I'm ahead, yes I am, you'll never catch me
It's a two feet lead, it's plain to see
I'll just look back to make quite sure
That I'll beat you this time, by more than a paw
Oh no you're gaining – this can't be real
If that's your breath on my tail I can feel
This is a shocker and it seems I've lost track
I know I should never, ever look back
Now we're running neck and neck
And it's a tie again – oh what the heck!
Our racing results are the same every day
Even if at the start I tell you to 'stay'!
We were born together at the beginning
So neither of us will end up winning!
So it seems to me there's just one catch
We're the same size and age! We're an even match…

just
weight

I wish I could live in far outer space
Then my skin would fall back in the right place
Here on earth it's heavy and touches the ground
Unless I am running at a pace – at a bound…
It starts with my ears when my paws hit the deck
Then a flurry of skin arrives on my neck
The next step moves on and up go my lips
And my tummy ends up rolling back to my hips!
Mid-stride is the best as I float at a height
And for a second my body feels almost feather light
Then down it comes from eyebrows to jowl
It's enough to make any boy howl
I know it's not PC, and perhaps asking a lot
Please NASA take me where I can skip, jump and trot!

now
you see me

I crept out of home at very first light
To see if I had got the message right
It said 'let's go play Hide and Seek
Until I count down, no one can peek!'
I already know the best place to hide
Even though size is not on my side!
My pulse pounds away as I sit dead still
This game always gives me the biggest thrill!
Hidden amongst the reeds and the bark
I hope they can't hear my racing heart?
I add a little something to aid my disguise
And brush down my fringe to hide my eyes
This is perfect – find me they won't
Now you see me – now you don't!

the win

Some say that I'm competitive at heart
So forget all that rubbish about just taking part!
I've got to be best at all that I do
Where my genes came from I haven't a clue
My Mum was relaxed and full of charm
My Dad is a trooper and works on a farm
I spend my time beating my own personal best
Happiest with a gold medal firmly on my chest
I race every day and give a hundred percent
I run and I run until I'm totally spent
I wait on the line for the count three, two, one
And get away like a bullet from a gun
The reason behind my huge medal yield?
It's simple – I'm the only one in the field!

and finally

Here are some shots from along the way
Taken in the south on more than one day
Thank you furry friends – for everything you do
And here's to your first book – all squeaky and new
Some on the beach, some on the park
We've all had a ball – it's been a right lark
Here at HQ I hope you love the book
And if you do – let your friends have a look
And if they are down it will give them a lift
A laugh always helps if you get my drift?
Maybe for Christmas or a special birthday?
As Time for Paws is a perfect give away!
Here's to our dogs of now and then…
…that's made me think – I'll grab my pen!

Lightning Source UK Ltd.
Milton Keynes UK
UKIC01n0828011213
222134UK00001B/14